BONNARD

Bonnard

by Raymond Cogniat

THE UFFICI PRESS - LUGANO

Title page: SELF-PORTRAIT, 1939-41
Canvas   Private Collection

Translated from the French by
ANNE ROSS

PRINTED IN ITALY

RIGHTS OF REPRODUCTIONS A.D.A.G.P. AND S.P.A.D.E.M., PARIS

ALL RIGHTS RESERVED

THE HOUSE AT TOURELLE, c. 1888   Canvas, 7½″ × 11½″   Private Collection

HIS AGE

Each time I have reason to write about Bonnard I feel a strange mixture of hesitation and pleasure, without being sure which is uppermost.   At first glance it seems that Bonnard needs to be explained less than any other painter, because one experiences his work with the exuberance of an encounter with something which captivates one without the need for analysis.   What is there to say, except to advise one's readers to yield to his magic?   Nevertheless it is always satisfying to discuss something one loves, whether to repeat the same words and ideas in order to recapture the inner vibrations set in motion by a work, or to become even better acquainted with the mechanism which, as soon as one tries to analyze it, shows an unsuspected complexity beneath its apparent simplicity — a simplicity which can probably be attributed to the fact that in his life, as in his work, Bonnard always represented his time and his social background, even when he seemed to clash with them, for at those moments he was helping to explain them through means one can instinctively perceive rather than rationally explain.

Everyone's life is of course significant of its time, and contributes to defining a society, if only because it is itself conditioned by that society, and from this standpoint the life of a petty official is as significant as that of an artist. If one therefore views an artist's work purely as a reflection of his life, and examines it only in that light, aesthetic merit and artistic quality become of secondary importance. A bad painting can be more effective than a good one to illustrate episodes in the artist's life. When a work of art surpasses this function of identification of an epoch by virtue of its own quality, it enters the ranks of the artistic hierarchy.

Bonnard deserves to be studied from both points of view. He is one of France's greatest painters of any period, but also a man among men of his own century, whose work should be regarded as belonging to that era before one determines its own independent character. This is only a point of departure, because it is essentially in its independence that his art captures our interest and our emotions. One must however bear in mind that these two strands in Bonnard are intricately interwoven.

From the topical level on which Bonnard represents the art of a society, one moves on to acknowledge him as one of the painters who *best* illustrate and reveal certain artistic currents. There are many and varied ways of defining an epoch: Modigliani, Picasso, Chagall and Utrillo said very contradictory things about the same period, and yet each in his own way provided an accurate image of the contemporary spirit. This they did through revolt or submission, pride or humility, vacillation or self-assurance. Each artist is like one face in a multiple portrait, a face whose features stand out the more when its painter is aggressively involved in his work and asserts his originality — that is, stresses his dissimilarity from others. Because Bonnard did not seek distinction, he attained it by indirect, yet simple means: he took the path of radical change and may be described as a bold revolutionary, yet he derived his inspiration from familiar, intimate things which to other people seem mundane features of everyday existence.

Bonnard lived and worked during a period of perhaps the most important changes in our civilization. The last quarter of the nineteenth century saw the rise of an unostentatious, discriminating middle-class, confident in a future which seemed to offer them the promise of lasting success. In the course of the century this middle-class had gained control of politics, industry, commerce and science, had developed a sincere taste for the arts and a strong belief in its own clear judgment. It was less and less inclined for revolutionary escapades, from which however it had benefited ever since the French Revolution, and to which to a great extent it owed its rise. It expected art to provide it with the reflection and confirmation of its own well-being, and not the provocative romanticism of men trying to

*Misia Godebska
1895   Charcoal
on card
15½" × 10¾"
National Museum
of Modern Art
Paris*

7

assert their own originality. Paradoxically, this epoque simultaneously saw the fermentation of this civil liberty which had been perpetually in jeopardy ever since it was first theoretically conceded at the end of the eighteenth century, for the stream of reforms promised thereafter were ineptly put into practice. Countless artists were to emerge from this cultured society, which however was surprised by the innovations of the best of them, and often rejected their work because it demonstrated a taste for this freedom which the artists had acquired, and to which they were all the more dedicated because their material situation had improved to the extent of allowing them at least a partial escape from their previous limitations.

This is a strange paradox: middle-class artists with middle-class resources in emotional and spiritual conflict with all the ideas and tastes of their background. Manet, Corot, Monet, Cézanne, Sisley, Gauguin, Seurat and Pissarro all came from the bourgeoisie, like Ingres, Delacroix, Chassériau and Géricault. Even when they thought they were escaping from it, it was the middle-class which provided their public. Bonnard and his friends were no exceptions to this rule, and hence they sought isolation in which to develop their ideas on art.

From then on the most vivid expressions of artistic creativity concerned activities away from the mainstream of life, disregarding the ardour, enthusiasm, even snobbism which gave birth to a limited but active public, ready to support artists in their most daring enterprises.

The lure of adventure and uncertainty among men satiated with tradition and stability is an instinctive defence against the threat of being engulfed. For years the avantgarde had been introducing subversive ideas to this peace-loving bourgeoisie, and one can see a militant tendency towards anarchy growing up beside conservative tradition, and in literary and artistic circles being translated from theory into action.

The avantgarde which began to promulgate artistic daring between 1900 and 1914 was a consequence of non-conformist influence. As the artist at the beginning of this century became more and more independent and isolated, two trends were developing simultaneously — the assertion of the individual, and the incomprehension of the public. Daring became provocation, provocation fed fashion, fashion made for swift and fleeting successes. As this rhythm acclelerated it gave an impression of disorder, and in its stormy wake brought some very uneven values, from which only a few exceptional personalities were later to emerge.

It might seem impossible in these conditions to pursue a career on the fringe of such chaos. Despite their revolutionary appearance, the new schools, from neo-impressionism to cubism, were built on theories under the pretext of re-establishing order. How could one live and work without becoming involved in battles of ideology or publicity? Some artists however found a means of defining their age by a very excess of peculiarity and by the fact that they moved within no current, did not invoke the authority of their elders and attracted no disciples. The first quarter of this century was therefore especially favourable

THE REVIEW, 1890
Canvas, 11¾″ × 8¾″   Private Collection

Two Dogs, 1891
Canvas, 14¼″ × 15¼″ Southampton Art Gallery, Great Britain

10

THE CAT, 1894
Card
20″ × 13″
J. Spreiregen's
Collection

YOUNG PARTRIDGE, 1889 Canvas, 8¾″ × 6¼″ Private Collection

to the simultaneous birth of poverty and success, so that the " artiste maudit " became no longer an exception, but an all too common case.

Bonnard succeeded in avoiding all these categories. He was neither prophet nor disciple, victim of misunderstanding nor slave to success. However he remained closely bound to the world which was taking shape around him. He was in fact, though not explicitly, a recorder set by destiny like an instrument on a control panel to gauge and measure the phenomenons of our civilization. He personified the resplendence of a waning society, the perfection and richness of arts without a future, when a decaying organism seemed about to burst out into new bloom yet in fact remained inimitable — unsurpassed because of its very perfection.

This society collapsed with the 1914-18 war and during the years which followed Bonnard continued involuntarily to bear witness, record temperatures and in short to be, in spite of his own development, the focal point of stability to which all around him could be related. The contrast between the order and calm in his works and in the feelings they express on the one hand, and on the other the violence which characterized the avantgarde, showed the prevalent unease.

During the years leading up to 1914 this society tried to modernize itself without relinquishing privilege. Discovering the avantgarde movement it adopted it as a means of bringing an element of fantasy into convention. Young people mischievously surrounded themselves with new artists, some of whom they even " discovered ", and then incited them to displays of eccentricity. This situation became more marked after the war, enlivened by an appetite for life and an atmosphere of miraculous resurgence out of the anguish that France had recently endured. Living and decaying creations mingled in a strange amalgam in which respectability began to crumble and convention to dissolve. Some artists escaped this holocaust, being too occupied with expressing themselves; others found it stimulating and even fed the flames.

Bonnard belonged among those who found enough motivation for life in themselves to be impervious to external pressures. Because he was unaware of this tempest and because his own boldness was never aggressive, he rallied around him those who, having been forced out of their old rut, felt full of new energy without seeing the need for revolt. Bonnard both reassured them and satisfied their desire for change.

An obvious equation with political currents is to be found here. In art when the great collective movements such as cubism, fauvism and expressionism became international, they accepted the idea of schism and took on coarser forms in Eastern Europe, Germany and Russia, while in the secrecy of small cliques artists were competing among themselves to evolve the first doctrines from which abstract art was to spring.

Bonnard continued on his lonely, pioneering path, manifesting so clearly his own personal liberty that the avantgarde, once it recognized his qualities, made no attempt to absorb him. Throughout those years of high tension he preserved a calm which was probably largely due to his indifference towards the excesses around him.

13

In France society was soon to find balance and to expand, by refusing to see the size and importance of problems, by letting time provide temporary solutions and learning to enjoy each moment as it came, while in other countries the most violent political developments were taking place. Bonnard's artistic refuge in fact went deeper than mere apparent resignation. His enclosed world seemed reassuring, but he often struck unexpected chords like warnings, signals of deeper, inner turmoil.

In 1940 the Second World War definitively destroyed the structure of the past, which gave

Tea in the Garden at Cannet, 1925   Pencil, 8½″ × 9½″   Private Collection, Paris

View of Paris — Montmartre   Pencil   Private Collection

Bonnard complete freedom, because from then on it was impossible to connect him with any of the great streams which were clashing or mingling to produce new artistic disciplines. Having lain hidden between the two wars, ardently developing its first experiments, abstract art now burst violently on the scene. It immediately grew to astonishing dimensions, not only through the enthusiasm of young artists burning to experiment, but also through the unexpected size of the public it attracted.

On the other side a movement towards social realism launched an attempt to introduce into art the ferments of political ideology and human predicament. Between these two extremes, the tranquil sophistication of the years of peace, which began to be called " poetic realism ", was relegated to obscurity. A new public, curious about the contemporary scene, entered the lists, armed however only with a very recently acquired knowledge which either neglected or despised all but the newest manifestations.

Only a few great names and great pre-war reputations emerged from the recent past to take on the character of " grand old men " — acknowledged masters who yet had only a limited influence. This group included Matisse, Rouault, Braque, Dufy and also Bonnard, whose native milieu was now so totally transformed that it had practically speaking disappeared and entered the realm of history.

HIS LIFE

Some men lead impenetrably secret, and therefore seemingly uneventful lives if they never show or speak of what fills their days and their minds. To pretend to understand a personality by enumerating his public actions, his friends, his external appearance and his travels is like presuming to understand his painting by listing his portraits, landscapes and still-lifes. If one is content with superficiality one will never learn about even the most apparently simple things.

Bonnard's painting, light yet opaque, completely fills the surface of the canvas, leading one to assume that his thoughts were also very full and complex and that one would never penetrate their inner meaning because it was enclosed in a gentle politeness which decisively discouraged importunity.

He was born on 3rd October, 1867 at Fontenay-aux-roses. His father came from Dauphiny and was an official in the Ministry of War. His childhood was uneventful and his upbringing wisely conducted to lead him towards a responsible, secure adulthood. As a child he studied well, moving in the traditional gradation from one school to the next, from Vauves to Louis-le-Grand and then to Charlemagne, taking his baccalauréat and then entering the university, which he left in 1887 with a degree in law. His docility did not however indicate a total contentment, because he simultaneously enrolled at the Julian Academy and thereafter for a year at the Fine Arts School. He did not seem to embark on his career as a painter with a feeling of obeying the call of an inescapable vocation. In the course of an interview he said to me:

" I am not sure whether the word ' vocation ' exactly applies to me. At that time I had not quite realized that I wanted to be a painter. I think that what attracted me then was less art itself than the artistic life, with all that I thought it meant in terms of free expression of imagination and freedom to live as one pleased. Of course I had been attracted by painting and drawing for a long time, without this becoming an irresistible passion; at any cost however I wanted to escape from a monotonous existence."

GARDEN UNDER SNOW, AT DUSK, 1910
Canvas, 23¼″ × 22½″   Private Collection

17

MADEMOISELLE
ANDRÉE BONNARD
WITH HER DOGS, 1890
Canvas, 74″ × 31½″
André Terrasse's Collection
Paris

LUNCHEON OR DESSERT, c. 1899
Wood, 11½″ × 13½″   Dr. A. Wilhelm's Collection, Bottmingen

PORTRAIT OF GEORGE BESSON, 1909 Canvas, 29½″ × 20¾″ George Besson's Collection

Portrait of a Young Girl, 1942   Pencil Drawing   Bowers Collection

The Little Laundress
1896   Charcoal
12¼" × 8"
Private Collection
Paris

22

The lure of a bohemian life which seems to have determined Bonnard's future career was typical of his time and his milieu — the product of an essentially middle-class attitude. The characters in Murger's picturesque portrait did not only represent the way of thinking and dreaming of certain young people in the middle of the century, for their idea that a world of the imagination was essential to life was to be developed during succeeding generations. Their heroes themselves came from middle-class families. The real poor, the proletariat, have never desired this pseudo-fantasy, because they know poverty is not freedom. A bohemian life is only tolerable when one has in the background the means to escape the anguish of incurable poverty.

Annette Vaillant has aptly summarized the duality of Bonnard's life: " bourgeois by birth but revolutionary in his painting, Bonnard led a bohemian life in a bourgeois way, moving from one house to another, from a barely furnished flat to an empty studio, to a hotel room, letting the years slip by and the seasons come and go ". This way of life demands the courage not to depend on anyone else — a courage which Bonnard demonstrated throughout his life.

Although this choice seemed more like an attempt to escape than a decree of fate, the course of Bonnard's future was already plotted from the beginning, and the stage set for the development of his personality. At the Julian Academy and at the School of Fine Arts he made friends with those who were to have a decisive influence on him — Vuillard, Roussel, Sérusier, Maurice Denis, Ibels and Vallotton.

The Julian Academy was primarily a centre for lively discussion among young people evolving new systems. One day in 1888, Sérusier returned from a vacation in Brittany with a painting he had made on wood at the instigation of Gauguin, whom he had just met. It was a landscape, the *Bois d'Amour* (*Wood of Love*) near Pont Aven, for which Gauguin had suggested the frank use of bright colours, maximum simplification of form and an intensity concentrated in the whole rather than in the details. There was such a powerful, convincing lesson to be learned from this picture, and it made such a strong impression on the young artists who saw it, that they called it among themselves " The Talisman ".

From these friendly meetings and vehement discussions sprang a desire to create a less tenuous and more explicitly unified group — an impulse which must be seen in its historical context. Symbolism was on the wane, numbers of small cliques were springing up, a revival of religious feeling was inspiring many groups of artists, young people were uniting to lend strength to their ideas, Gauguin was dreaming of founding a studio with his disciples in the tropics — at Madagascar or Tahiti — Van Gogh was also thinking of starting a collective workshop at Arles, Verkade, after belonging to the Pont Aven group, had gone into a monastery, Maurice Denis yearned to resuscitate religious art, the Rosicrucians hoped to lead painters and poets towards a revival of mystical initiation rites and Gustave Moreau was witnessing the triumph of his pagan mythology.

In this atmosphere it was often difficult to distinguish the genuine from the bogus, and so the group of young painters of the Julian Academy felt the need to assert to themselves

*Standing Nude
with
Self-Portrait
of Bonnard's
Face, 1930
Charcoal
23½" × 18"
Private
Collection
Paris*

▷

THE TUB, 1920
Canvas
50½" × 31"
Private
Collection

WOMAN WITH PARROT, 1916
Canvas, 41″ × 48″   Private Collection

AMBROISE VOLLARD, c. 1906
Canvas, 29¼″ × 36¼″   Art Museum, Zürich, Switzerland

28

Street Scene
1920-25
Pencil
8¾″ × 5½″
Victor
Waddington
llection, London

their autonomy and ideological cohesion and to draw up a plan of action. On his return from Brittany Sérusier had already started the new group, and remained its driving force. His romanticism, religious feeling, taste for mystery — perhaps even more his sense of humour — led him to suggest that the group should call themselves " nabis ", which he said was Hebrew for " prophet ", because they proclaimed a new artistic gospel. They knew they had much to learn and almost everything still to discover, because at that time sources of information were very limited and even recent events were often partly or wholly unknown. In the same interview from which I quoted above Pierre Bonnard said to me: " I remember very well that at that time I knew nothing about impressionism and we admired Gauguin's work for itself and not in its context. Besides, when we discovered impressionism a little later, it came as a new enthusiasm, a sense of revelation and liberation, because Gauguin is a classic, almost a traditionalist, and impressionism brought us freedom."

I have found another important definition in the same text. When I asked Bonnard whether he remembered the exact moment of crystallization of his own style, he replied " during a holiday I spent in about 1895 in Dauphiny, at a house belonging to my family. One day, all the words and theories which formed the basis of our conversations — colour, harmony, the relationship between line and tone, balance — seemed to have lost their abstract implication and become concrete. In a flash I understood what I was looking for and how I could set about achieving it ".

Bonnard was too modest in naming 1895 as the significant year, because many of his earlier works which we now know bear the unmistakable stamp of his personality. It is true that they also, and more urgently, belong to the collective trend which we shall consider later, and which is one of the aspects of the " Modern Style " prevalent around the end of the century.

From the moment he entered the Julian Academy Bonnard had definitely abandoned the idea of becoming a lawyer. In 1889 he sold his first poster and settled into a studio at the Batignolles. In 1890 he made friends with Vuillard and Maurice Denis and the three young men jointly rented a studio in Rue Pigalle, where through his companions he met Lugné Poe, André Antoine and Paul Fort. In the same year his sister married a musician, Claude Terrasse, and so Bonnard began to settle into a circle of artists not exclusively concerned with painting, but also with literature, drama and poetry and the relationships between the various genres.

During the same year of 1890 an exhibition of Japanese art at the School of Fine Arts impressed him greatly and contributed as much as the " Modern Style " to forming his technique. The following year saw him exhibiting for the first time at the Salon des Indépendants, with nine paintings, and he also took part in the nabis' exhibition at the gallery of Le Barc de Boutteville. Contemporary furniture, textiles and screens showed that painters were not only concerned with making pictures, but also with making painting a harmonious part of the decorative arts. Further exhibitions in 1892 at the Salon des Indépendants

THE RACES, 1894
Water-colour, 7½″ × 7¼″   Paul Mellon's Collection, U.S.A.

31

32

and Le Barc de Boutteville decisively extablished Bonnard's place in the artistic world, for critics such as Roger-Marx, Gustave Geffroy and Albert Aurier commented on his work. "La Revue Blanche", founded in 1889 in Liège, found its way to Paris in 1891. Its directors, the brothers Alexandre and Thadée Natanson, gathered around them during the thirteen years of the journal's existence (until April, 1903) many and varied writers and painters, who shared a sense of unostentatious humanity, considerable, unaffected discrimination and an aesthetic sensitivity to life around them. They were all decisive, independent and severely critical without ferocity; in short, they had an instinct for basic originality and moderation which already characterized Bonnard and his friends, who were all suited to participate in such a movement. This coterie of the "Revue Blanche" was precisely that of the sohpisticated, radical bourgeoisie which we have already mentioned, and which combined contradictory trends of social comfort and emotional dissatisfaction. Bonnard never again found a realm more suited to his nature, and its imprint remained with him for the rest of his life.

In 1893 he started his career as an illustrator with two works by Claude Terrasse, *Les Petites Scènes Familières* and *Le Petit Solfège* (*Little Family Scenes* and *The Little Tonic Sol-fa*). One could even attempt to define Bonnard by the writers he knew or illustrated. In fact he was more to be found in company with writers than painters, for his friendships depended on his private feelings rather than on his working relationships. He illustrated works by Jules Renard, Verlaine, Mirbeau, Colette and Longus, he contributed to the "Revue Blanche", and some years later to the "Cahiers d'Aujourd'hui" ("Contemporary Studies") edited by George Besson, where his drawings illustrated texts by the same authors, in company with works by Renoir and Marquet.

What did these men have in common? A desire to look at life and to reproduce it, to find the genuine emotion behind every image, to seek a truth rather than adhere to an aesthetic system but also to reach this truth by apparently simple ways which were in fact deeply original. Whether stern or indulgent, ironical or austere, all these middle-class radicals felt a certain gentleness towards man, his little troubles and peccadilloes, and the deeper significance of that which others thought banal. As a result they all refused to make their names through a display of virtuosity, because they believed that the essence of art lay not in originality of form but in the way in which form expressed the secret reality of each moment of life.

There is little else to say. In 1894 Bonnard met Maria Boursin, who subsequently served as model (Marthe) for nearly all his paintings, and whom he married in 1925. Here the story of his life may be concluded. Creation and evolution had blended together and every event which was to determine his future had already occurred. The remainder of the story — at least so far as we know it — is told in the exhibitions at Vollard's, Bernheim's and Druet's: his gradual climb to success and fame, his patient, continuous work, his book illustrations, his ratification by the acceptance of his works by the galleries. One should also mention his discovery of the South of France in about 1910, and in 1925 his

*A Woman
of Elegance
1924
Charcoal
9″ × 6″
Private
Collection
London*

CHILDREN IN THE GARDEN
Pastel   Richard Bühler's Collection, Winterthur, Switzerland

purchase of a house at Cannet, where on 23rd January, 1947, he died, Marthe having died there in 1942.

Yet this uneventful life was significant. It followed the slow rhythmic dance of a destiny which over three-quarters of a century had like many others succeeded in avoiding the violence of abrupt political change, while yet absorbing it and reflecting the mundane stages of human existence.

One could divide this span into three great periods. The first comprised the years of ap-strenticeship, his enriching friendships and his capture of the object of his search, the Julian Academy, the formation of the friendly group of nabis, the " Revue Blanche " and the expounding of theories. The second was that of the years of consolidation, for from the turn of the century, as we have seen, the die was already cast for Bonnard. He deliberately restricted himself to his immediate surroundings in order to preserve his independence. The third period, from 1920 on, was that of solitude — not the solitude of a victim or a misanthropist, but a voluntary, unaffected solitude which is an uncompromising form of freedom.

HIS WORK

The uniformity of Bonnard's work is so marked despite its variety, and his early and late paintings are so closely related that this seems to be more a continuity of artistic inspiration than of technique. If one could interpret his painting, it would certainly reveal his character in its entirety, because he thought and felt every work so intensively before he actually realized it. While most modern artists find their stimulus in the continual discovery of and experimentation with new means of expression, because they are afraid of repeating themselves, Bonnard almost seemed to curb his ambition and to enclose himself in his own circumscribed world. Throughout his life he was perpetually working on the same themes and the same details, not — like the impressionists — to capture the passing hour or season, but rather in obedience to an inner desire to record a range of modulation, colour and harmony.

The main difference between the impressionists and Bonnard was that they sought to seize a passing moment while he had no such compulsion, and his art was not concerned with their attention to immediate, mobile reality. If he did to a certain extent seize the ephem-eral nature of a subject, and if his painting in fact had the necessary lightness of touch, this arose neither from a wish to perpetuate what is temporary nor from a satisfaction with transient emotion, but from a desire to discover the lasting element in this fleetingness. Impermanence lay in the themes themselves and the mood they exuded, not in the paint-er's eye, for he painted women, flowers, youth and nature.

In spite of his concern with impermanence, he succeeded in giving places, beings and things a semblance of stability without stylization, even when he was briefly influenced by the

THE CHALETS, 1930
Water-colour, 4½" × 6¼"   Private Collection, Montreal, Canada

▷

THE FRENCH WINDOW, 1930
Water-colour, 6" × 4½"   Bowers Collection

40

THE LUNCHEON
1922
Canvas
26½″ × 14¾″
Private
Collection

NUDE IN THE BATH
1917
Canvas, 31½″ × 17¼″
Alphonse Bellier's
Collection, Paris

NUDE WITH LAMP, c. 1910
Canvas, 30″ × 29½″ Professor Hans R. Hahnloser's Collection, Bern, Switzerland

PASTORAL, 1916-20
Canvas, 51½″ × 64¼″   Bernheim-Jeune Collection

44

systems of the "Modern Style". With Bonnard one never has the impression of being presented with an *a priori* accepted idea, and without seeming improvized, each canvas has obviously been painted slowly, with successive additions, patient retouching and reflection, like the opening of a flower or the ripening of a fruit. In this slow way each picture seems complete and finished without being immobile, and one can understand that a scrupulous man like Bonnard often needed to add some new emphasis or new touches of colour to old canvases.

His concern for improvement did not mar his serenity. One cannot detect in his works the tormenting disquiet of an unsatisfied artist obsessed with the desire to outstrip himself. He did not try to keep up to date, yet he never repeated himself. Even with a subject he had already used, he created a new picture with such subtle differences that it would be impossible to copy one of his works exactly. His unobtrusiveness and his modesty saved him from discontent because he did not try to step outside his own medium and capacity.

He was content with what lay within his reach, and through his good taste, culture, lyrical feeling and even naïvety, his works have a human quality to which less scrupulous and vainer ambitions could never have led. One can detect not the smallest affectation in him in either his pursuit of pleasure or his asceticism, but this instinct for moderation never even led him to use mediocre means of expression.

A Bonnard picture makes one think of a fruit or a flower because of its texture, colour, charm and the earthy sensuality it exudes. It awakens all one's senses, even evoking a feeling of music. One wants to pick the flower and smell its perfume. It is always the same and always new, like all flowers and fruit, similar yet subtly different, imbued each time with a new freshness and a new joy in living at the moment of its loveliest metamorphosis. This is probably how he obtains this inner feeling of impermanence which we have just mentioned, and which is so different from the external impermanence of the impressionists. Bonnard's art stands at the ill-defined frontier between painting and poetry, which by the simplest means it succeeds in crystallizing.

If one tries to analyze the component parts of his work and to examine his attitude to the problems of composition, perspective, colour and draftsmanship, one must above all remember his position in relation to his predecessor, impressionism. We have seen that he did not realize its existence until he had completed several years of study, and that he knew nothing about it when he first began to paint. When he first took an interest in Gauguin's experiments he was embarking on a course which without his realizing it was a reaction against impressionism, and his later admiration for that movement could not eliminate the traces of his first tendency. This initial contradiction characterized his whole life's work, which can be regarded as both an extension of and an escape from impressionism.

This complex attitude explains to a great extent the nature of his austere yet flexible composition. He belonged to the generation which preceded cubism, and was beginning to be concerned with the need to restore deliberate structure to painting and, without falling into

"My Caravan" at Vernonnet, 1930
Water-colour, 13¾" × 17"   Mr. Charles Zadok's Collection, New York

THE MEDITERRANEAN, 1930
Gouache, 10″ × 11¼″ Private Collection, London

the rigid geometry which cubism was to propound, tried to establish a framework and to hint at the deliberate purpose behind a composition rather than accepting the haphazard harmonies of direct observation.

Many times in the course of his life Bonnard seems to have been moved by a need for order, but being unself-conscious he did not systematically yield to this urge. Though often one can easily discern the geometric pattern on which he based the arrangement of the various elements in a picture, this geometry is always camouflaged and can only be discovered by those who deliberately look for it. It is part of realism, to be found in the frame of a mirror, door or window, or the surface of a table, which all divide a canvas into large rectangles. Sometimes even a horizontal line creates a rough barrier across a whole picture, whether it is the distant edge of the sea, a windowsill or the border of a mirror. In this case they are not just casual rectangles thrown together, but horizontal bands to divide the picture into parallel zones.

In other cases Bonnard adds the massive diagonals of a half-open door or window to enliven or break up the monotony of these rhythms. The straight lines which make up the patterns are softened by the texture of the painting so that they become a hidden structural element. This concealed severity restores stability to the liberties he takes with space, if only because it serves to decentralize the principal subject of the picture, whether a person, a tree or an inanimate object, and here one can see another example of the Japanese influence visible also in the works of Dégas and Lautrec.

This taste for contrast resulting from harmonious interplay of planes leads him to alter dimensions and proportion, and one cannot believe this is just a matter of chance. When he was commissioned to paint a panel for the foyer of the theatre in the Palais de Chaillot, he said frankly: " they gave me a square and I managed to destroy it ", which shows his desire not to be governed by arbitrary geometrical form.

It seems that Bonnard took a certain pleasure in tackling and even creating difficulties of this kind, by using canvases of strange dimensions, either very long or very broad, like the panels of the screens which often feature in his work. In normal-sized canvases he frequently introduced partitions to divide his composition into compartments of different sizes, each containing independent subjects, and then, having made these divisions, he succeeded in giving a unity to the whole, not simply through style but also through the actual relationships between the different zones.

Bonnard's intriguing geometry is his own personal manipulation of space, however without his intending that it should serve as a trick of perspective capable of destroying the unity of a surface. One must start from this idea of geometrical structure, diffused yet perceptible, to explain Bonnard's use of perspective and to understand its originality.

★　★　★

Perspective is the sum of the technical rules accepted by an artist to suggest a third dimension on a two-dimensional surface. It is his means of constructing space, while respecting certain conventions which belong especially to his trade. Bonnard's idea of space

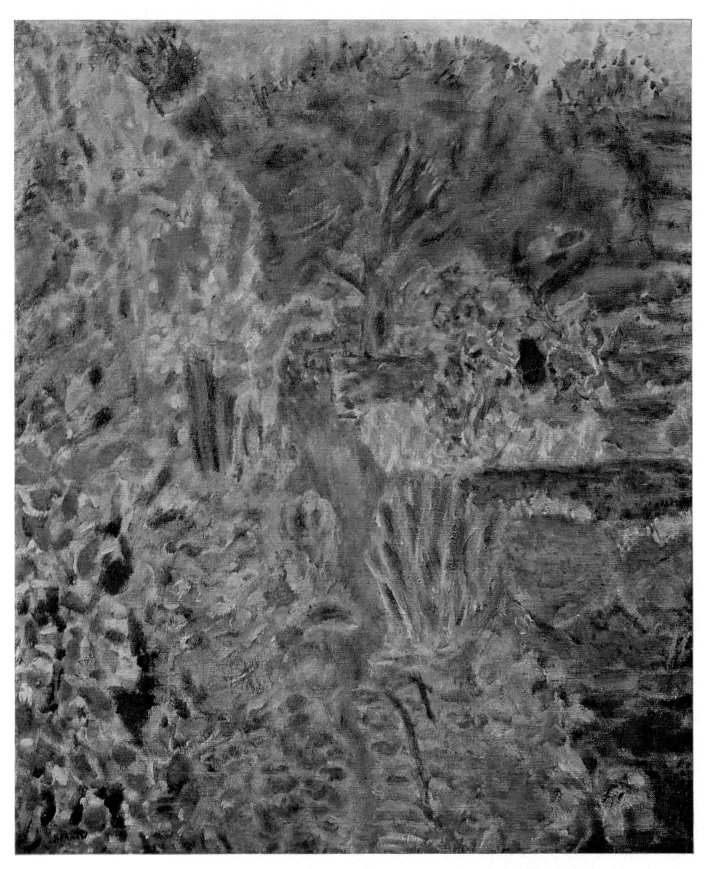

The Garden at Cannet, 1943   Canvas, 26¼″ × 21¾″   Private Collection

THE LATEEN SAIL, 1917
Canvas, 17" × 26½" Bernheim-Jeune Collection

THE SEINE, c. 1930
Canvas, 15½" × 22¼" Private Collection

▽

WILD FLOWERS, c. 1916   Canvas, 29¼″ × 21¾″   Private Collection

is wholly his own, independent of other concepts, even when his processes seem borrowed. It is as different from that of the Japanese as it is from the geometrical perspective adopted and exploited in western art in all its ramifications ever since the Renaissance.

This last-named perspective tries to give as much impression of depth and thrust in the furthest distance as possible, while the line of the horizon stresses vanishing diagonals to give an illusion of reality to the third dimension and to detach each object from its surroundings. This desire to create relief was carried so far that from it derived trompe-l'œil, and it is the tradition in western art to distort every detail in order to obtain the maximum effect of relief.

Bonnard however avoided this kind of simulation. As we have seen, horizontal lines often dominate his composition, organized in a certain rhythm by means of a series of parallel bands facing the spectator. When diagonals intrude, as they often do with simulated force, they serve not to stress the distance between planes, but to telescope them. Instead of expanding space, Bonnard contracts it to the point where relief is eliminated and no single feature is isolated from its surroundings. This does not lead to flat, monotonous surfaces as in Japanese prints, for Bonnard does not freeze and stratify his limited universe by crystallizing the air, as oriental artists seem to do. On the contrary his world quivers with life through a concentration of infinite vibrations, like the buzzing of bees in a hive, and his form does not depend on the contour of an object as traditional painting teaches us, nor on its relief, but on its luminous radiation.

In this concentration distance approaches us and enters our immediate surroundings, while the horizon, instead of giving breathing space to the structure of a landscape, closes it within a coloured frame, both light and impenetrable, mobile and opaque. This obvious wish to reduce space so far as possible is proved by his use of windows and mirrors. In both cases the interplay consists of juxtaposing and contrasting two clearly differentiated planes, in order to dislocate the painting and vary the relationships within it. A Bonnard window never forms a hole in the middle of the foreground, to draw the eye away from the principal part of the picture, but rather brings the distance nearer, in an attempt to harmonize and blend it with the foreground.

This feeling of absorption of space is even more noticeable because of Bonnard's frequent use of mirrors. If one thinks of Manet's *Bar at the Folies Bergères* or of Van Eyck's double portrait of the Arnolfinis, to take two famous examples of the use of mirrors, one can see how they create new dimensions in an enclosed space, lengthening and even multiplying distance until they almost give an impression of infinity. Bonnard achieves a diametrically opposite result; his mirrors serve to close the world of the picture completely on the spectator, not allowing his imagination to play on the emptiness behind him, which is already filled, circumscribed by the mirror's frame, and irrevocably incorporated into the painting. The spectator is forceably imprisoned at the centre of a fluid world, from which there is no escape. This overlapping of planes, with no outlines around the objects and no lines disappearing into the distance or sculpted by shadow, is yet lucid. A certain order of spatial

BASKET OF FRUIT, 1930
Gouache, 11″ × 15″   Madame Marianne Feilchenfeldt's Collection, Zürich, Switzerland

54

FRUIT (PALE HARMONY), c. 1930   Water-colour and gouache, 13¾″ × 12½″   Private Collection

values is in fact created by the relative dimensions of the elements of the picture. Thus in the foreground are most often to be found objects of huge dimensions compared with what lies immediately behind them. So Bonnard arrives at a perceptible order which gives rhythm to the extremely complex zones which fill his space, and verisimilitude to what would otherwise lack it. He often adopts a vertical perspective with the horizontal plane stood on end, in order to stress the predominance of the foreground. For instance, in some still-lifes or interiors he makes the surface of a table occupy the whole of the picture, with his people relegated like accessories to the very top of the canvas.

★ ★ ★

Through studying his use of colour one can best follow the stages of Bonnard's development, because through colour he expressed his contact with the outer world and gave his feelings a physically perceptible form. Colour, regarded as a substance, facilitates and simplifies the demonstration of emotion, sensuality, timidity or intimacy, which can thus be naturally expressed, while draftsmanship or composition introduce less totally instinctive factors.

His earliest known pictures, dating from 1886-88, are still somewhat impersonal, but one can see that Bonnard already had a touch which could make colour vibrate, and could fragment it without dividing it into distinct shades. From 1890 he became more conscious of his quest, and one might assume that from then on, after the contacts he made at the Julian Academy, he entered into a system and became susceptible to influence, though as an act of acceptance, not of submission. Probably this was his way of subscribing to a discipline which rid him of banality, and through which he could discover a way to escape from uncertainty and clichés, while finding in it a starting point for his own experiences.

At this distance of time we can now see that in these years he hinted at all the elements which were to compose his mature personality: the importance of volume in the foreground, decentralized compositions, contraction of space, density of atmosphere, suppleness and as often as possible the elimination of a distant horizon. From this moment on one could predict that colour was to blur the outlines of his shapes and their volumes and that the unity of a picture would spring from colour because it softened structural severity.

At the Julian Academy and with the nabis Bonnard by no means accepted blindly the doctrine brought to Paris from Pont-Aven by Sérusier in 1888, neither can one distinguish Gauguin's influence on his work at this time, but rather the sign of the times themselves, that is, the lure of that " Modern Style " which required an artist to reinvent reality in order to embellish daily life — a blend of sophistication, artificiality and a return to nature, conditional however on imposing on her certain arbitrary rhythms. Bonnard contributed

something much simpler than the fashionable elaborate, contrived arabesques to this subtly complex art; he went quite naturally beyond theories and looked around him, which is surely the best way to be a modern. He painted his surroundings, his family and his friends with deep affection.

In spite of the attraction of Japanese art — his friends called him " the Japanesque nabi " — he did not apply his colour in a smooth coat but in visible strokes, not attempting to suggest thereby the shimmering and transitory nature of light as did the impressionists, but to make simplified surfaces more vibrant.

Soon his observation of street scenes was to change his range of colours and the arrangement of his compositions. Constrasts appeared more frequently, and with more emphasis. Black became a favourite colour, especially in his paintings of the Boulevard de Clichy at night. Earlier influences on his work gradually faded, thus proving that they had only ever been ways of escape. They were outdated even before Bonnard had found his definitive style, when one could still sense much uncertainty and awkwardness in his work.

Nevertheless, taking into account what was to follow, one may be allowed to believe that from then on Bonnard knew — or at least guessed — how he would develop, not with the aggressive certainty of a conqueror proud of his youth and his gifts and sure of himself, but with the calm determination arising from knowledge of his own capabilities, even if these had not yet reached their full maturity. It seems that he never sought mechanical perfection, but always had a kind of naïvety which gives most of his canvases an air of improvization and almost deliberate casualness, which were in fact neither affected nor deliberate; they were unimportant, because he believed that the essence of his art lay elsewhere.

Harsh contrasts of colour which characterize his views of Paris by night show his talent for making uncompromising contrasts acceptable. He could create an atmosphere of intense colour with a limited palette or give a monochrome impression with a complex interplay of colours. One sees this better still in the subsequent years, when he returned to intimate subjects, family portraits and nudes in interiors enveloped in waves of grey dusk. From then on he was to alternate his themes, and one is hardly drawn to classify them too strictly chronologically, for they harmonize and complement each other through their very differences.

Bonnard's colour exudes such joy, as it moves harmoniously from the subdued vibrations of the turn of the century to the lavish splashes of his final years, he so ardently sought to avoid a lack of continuity and so often returned to a work after a gap of several years, to correct it and bring it into line with his new ideas, that it is easier to discuss his art with admiration than with a sense of history. Certainly in the course of the years he did acquire an amazing technique, and his canvases increasingly displayed a prodigious virtuosity, the demonstration of which was not however his aim; it served simply to give him greater freedom in expressing his intensely sensuous feelings.

Nude in Profile, 1920-30 Pencil, 12½″ × 9½″ Private Collection, Paris

Vase of Flowers Water-colour Private Collection

60

Woman Indoors Reading a Journal, 1925   Canvas, 57″ × 35¾″   Private Collection, New York

WOMAN WITH BLACK STOCKINGS or THE SHOE, 1900
Canvas, 24½″ × 25¼″   Rosengart Gallery, Lucerne, Switzerland

▷
WOMAN WITH BLACK STOCKINGS, c. 1900
Wood, 23¼″ × 17″   Lord Rosslyn's Collection, Great Britain

THE LUNCHEON, 1932
Canvas, 26¾″ × 32¾″   Petit Palais Museum, Paris

64

Thus he approached the realm of colour with complete emancipation, both from the traditions of his schooling and from subsequent ideas; in fact this unbiassed awareness which characterized his work and opened new doors to him also led him to obtain unexpected and unprecedented effects. By juxtaposing related shades, such as red and mauve, or orange and yellow, he achieved a visual vibration and a sharpness of impact which almost trouble one's eye, and are more violent than contrasts. Even in his series of intimate grisaille pictures the mixture of milky white, pinks or mauves give an effect of luminous iridescence instead of the chilly half-light one might expect.

This science of colour which led him to reconcile soft and bright harmonies, also enabled him to use strong colours without violence. His blazing reds and even his great expanses of dark blue or black make sombre or glowing areas of colour, always incorporated in a soft, velvety, mildly voluptuous whole which absorbs clashes.

This method of softening contrasts or enriching harmonies — that is, of seeking and attaining unaccustomed effects — reached its fullest expression in his back-lighting, which gives as luminous an effect as direct lighting. Bonnard understood the majesty of colour better than any other painter and the light which emanates from each shape and each figure is always projected to the uttermost. His intense lavishness is not the opposition of light and dark, or cool and warm shades, but exploration of the intensity of each component; that is, exaltation rather than opposition.

By this means Bonnard adopted in his own way Gauguin's theory as transmitted by Sérusier, that colour should be carried to the point of its maximum power. At all times he demanded of his pigment the function of a colouring agent and no other. His painting never tried to become a facsimile of matter, of wood or flesh, nor yet a spatial trompe l'œil, but just coloured texture. The only exceptions to this honesty are his scenes portrayed through a window or a mirror, where he gives physical form to the difference in sensation between a direct view and a reflection. In fact in this case he is conveying a difference of atmosphere rather than a difference of texture — inevitably, since he never copied reality but metamorphosed it in zones of colour. Through this metamorphosis he attained the transformation of space and distortion of planes of which we have already spoken.

★ ★ ★

If Bonnard's sensitivity and sensuality are embodied in colour, and his intelligence and the subtlety of his attitude to theory embodied in his composition, his way of capturing life and his unexpectedness lie at the heart of his draftsmanship, though it would not be right to take this demarcation of Bonnard's qualities too seriously and to believe in strict divisions between each of his media. It is however certain that his drawing shows a kind of humour not found in his painting, except in certain particular cases and always in a very tenuous form. Perhaps this is because painting, though it seems spontaneous and never

CORNER OF A
DINING-ROOM
c. 1930
Gouache
19¾″ × 12½″
Private
Collection
◁

▷
WHITE TRAY
c. 1930
Gouache
25¼″ × 19¾″
Private
Collection

forced, still demands care and even revision, and a clear use of the medium, while drawing is completely free and imposes no restraint.

Bonnard's humour never becomes caricature, for he has too much respect for humanity and too much benevolence to ridicule anything, but his observant spirit inevitably led him to smile. The characters in his drawings are never grotesque, and a proof that he lacks malice is that his humour is often directed at animals, especially dogs and cats, which he drew in very unusual attitudes. Another indication of gentle humour in his drawing can be found in the fact that most of his sketches are of his best and oldest friends.

Clearly drawing was not an end in itself for Bonnard, but just an amusing way of taking notes. Nowhere can one detect the effort behind a carefully applied stroke, because he usually drew as he painted, in tiny touches and indications. His drawings are only rarely

Little Girl with Dog, 1929   Graphite, 9¾" × 13½"   Private Collection

LITTLE GIRL WITH DOG, 1929-32
Canvas, 20″ × 24¾″   Private Collection, Fontainebleau, France

YELLOW NUDE
c. 1932
Canvas
31″ × 17¾″
Beyeler Gallery
Basle, Switzerland

DARK NUDE, 1941-44 Canvas, 31″ × 17″ Private Collection

CANNES - LA CROISETTE, c. 1925
Canvas, 10¾" × 21¼" Private Collection

THE PORT AT CANNES, 1930
Gouache, 11" × 15" Victor Waddington's Collection, London
▽

The Fruit-Picker
Pen and brush
drawing
Private Collection

Illustration for " Daphnis et Chloé ", 1902
Lithograph   Private Collection

STILL LIFE WITH FRUIT, c. 1935 Gouache, 12½″ × 19¼″ Maurice Coutot's Collection, Paris

studies for large pictures — at least so far as we know them — but executed more like jottings in a private language, as though just for his own eyes. In most cases one has a feeling that Bonnard's drawings were not intended for the public gaze, and when he did agree to part with some of them he did it out of kindness, because he had found enthusiasts who wanted to have them and whom he did not know how to refuse.

His engravings, and especially his lithographs, occupy a significant place in his output. They gave him an opportunity to use his gifts of draftsmanship to the full and were obviously intended for the public eye. To many artists who embrace this form after starting on their careers as painters, lithography seems just a means of duplicating copies of a painting, drawing or water-colour. They therefore try to adapt their painting style to the new process and treat stone like canvas or paper. Bonnard however first became known as a lithographer, his first known work being a poster for " France Champagne ", commissioned in 1889. It is said that on seeing this poster Toulouse-Lautrec first began to take an interest in the process and that Bonnard introduced him to Ancourt the printer, who soon after brought out the famous poster for the Moulin Rouge, to be followed by the amazing works one knows so well and which all resembled the style of his first effort.

Bonnard brought to the virtually unexplored realm of the illustrated poster a new tone, a feminine grace which in a way resembled that of Jules Chéret, the master of this medium, yet differed from the latter in the style of his draftsmanship and the restraint of his palette.

His second lithograph was a coloured print pulled in 1892 and in the same year he designed the cover for a book, *Reine de Joie* (*Queen of Joy*) by Victor Joze and a plate for the January-March 1893 number of a periodical called *L'Estampe Original* (*Original Prints*). One can see from these first attempts that Bonnard absorbed the influences which affected him and gave them his own personal flavour, but Claude Roger-Marx was right to recall Chéret when discussing *France Champagne*, and the Far East when discussing the other works.

Unlike his paintings, Bonnard's lithographs demonstrate a skill in the use of large flat areas of colour, and his very limited palette did not prevent his giving his compositions a luminous intensity and a great impression of vitality. This draftsmanship was noticeably different from his later style, and comprised extended strokes outlining his objects with an almost stylized emphasis and precision, whereas later he was to use disconnected strokes. Sometimes he would revert to his original simplicity and always showed great economy in his range of tone, succeeding in obtaining amazing luminosity, even with as few as three or four colours. In his use of letter-press Bonnard tried to break the mechanical pattern of typography, and to use a kind of flexible, uneven handwriting which would harmonize better with the illustration.

In 1893 appeared the first book illustrated by Bonnard, a collection of songs by Franc Nohain, set to music by Claude Terrasse and decorated with nineteen lithograph illustrations. From then on the engraver's technique merged with that of the painter, for his drawings were made with a series of tiny, supple lines — mere hints which scored the stone

Nude Standing, c. 1930
Graphite
28¾″ × 19¼″
Art Gallery
Bremen, W. Germany

and gave movement to the surface. This animation of planes was to remain one of Bonnard's prime concerns in engraving as much as in painting. He did however return to the large flat expanses of colour when seeking more decorative effects and in them recalled the lessons he had learned from Japanese art. Thus the poster for the " Revue Blanche " (1894) is a good example of broad monochrome surfaces used without severity, and also proves his skill in blending and balancing opposites in the same composition by adding a highly animated background to these unified surfaces, or by setting the text partially against a white background and without outline, partially with a black outline, without one feeling a break in the flow of the letters.

Bonnard's cover for the 1895 edition of the album of the " Revue Blanche " consisted simply of a black design, and his lithograph entitled *La Femme au Parapluie* (*Woman with Umbrella*) was just a black silhouette enlivened with a small pink mark. This Japanese influence reappears both in the composition and the colour of the prints published in 1897 for the albums of painter-engravers sponsored by Vollard, and even more distinctly in the four-panelled screen of 1899. This influence is also found in *La Maison dans la Cour* (*The House in the Courtyard*) — one of the plates in the volume published by Vollard in 1899 under the title *Quelques Aspects de la Vie de Paris* (*Some Views of Parisian Life*) — although in this plate he combined animated and flat surfaces.

It is interesting to study the close relationship, the analogies and the differences, between Bonnard's engraving and his painting as seen in a print entitled *Le Canotage* (*Canoeing*) and a painting on the same theme executed in 1896. In both works the composition is identical and Bonnard shows exceptional skill in obtaining a similar spatial vibration and an equally vivid sense of colour in both engraving and painting, even though the former is limited to the use of four colours.

Bonnard made few engravings of landscapes, but many street-scenes, showing his preference for urban sights and sounds — the teeming crowds of passers-by in the street contrasted with the vertical rigidity of the buildings. He often viewed the scene from above, which gave rise to the upright perspectives already mentioned in connection with his painting, and showed once more his affection for Eastern art. His interiors and his nudes were treated with that feeling of intimacy and protective silence which characterized his painting and allowed him to obtain in black and white the effects which could convey his sensitivity and naïve feeling of wonder when contemplating everyday life.

An important part of his engraving work consisted of book illustrations. To those already mentioned should be added *Le Petit Solfège* (1893) by Claude Terrasse, which he illustrated with drawings, and in particular several works which were mostly unsuccessful when they first appeared, but are now counted rightly among the greatest masterpieces of French bibliography of the turn of the century. These include a collection of Verlaine's poems called *Parallèlement* (*In Parallel*), illustrated with red chalk lithographs, including nudes of voluptuous tenderness without a shadow of vulgarity, followed by *Daphnis et Chloë* in 1902, in which the classical nudes seem through their gracefulness to lose any archaic appearance

ALMOND TREE IN BLOSSOM, 1946-7
Canvas, 21¾″ × 14½″ National Museum of Modern Art, Paris

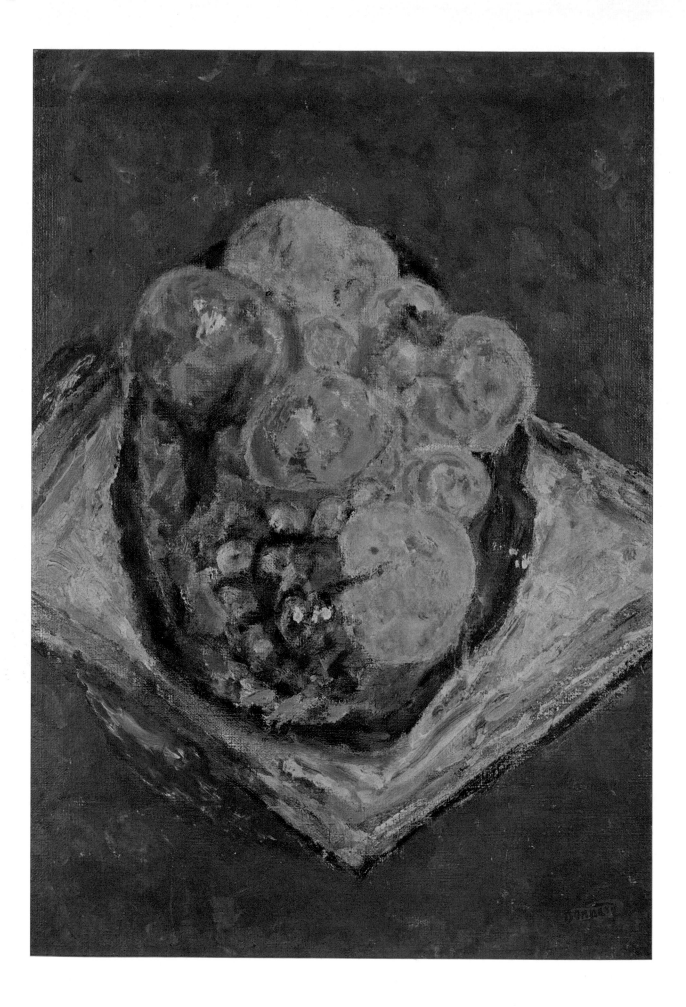

ROSES, 1943
Canvas, 14½″ × 15¾″ Mademoiselle Renée Terrasse's Collection, Paris

◁

PEACHES AND GRAPES, 1943
Canvas, 18″ × 29¼″ Private Collection

STILL LIFE
BONNARD'S
LAST PICTURE
1946 Canvas
Maeght Gallery
Paris

and to take their place in the timelessness of life. Other examples are *Les Histoires Naturelles* (*Natural History*) by Jules Renard, characterized by the painter's lively, ironical style, which can capture the movement of an instant, *Sainte Monique* by Vollard, with graceful, feminine etchings, *Simili*, by Claude Roger-Marx and two works by Mirbeau, *Dingo* and *La 628 E 8*.

CONCLUSION

Having tried to cover all the component parts of Bonnard's art one realizes with astonishment how rich and complex is his output, which seemed at first glance so simple, because one yields immediately to its charm without feeling the desire or need to analyze its mechanism. One must stand back from the charm in order to penetrate it in depth and uncover the variety and originality of the methods he uses more or less consciously. In fact his work is so spontaneous that it is hard to believe in a systematic application of theory, and thus, when relating causes and effects, establishing his principles and the absence of any declaration of intention in his writings or his conversation, one is led to speak of naïvety, even though we know how skilful and cerebral his art really was.

He never used his technique to demonstrate his mastery, because he did not feel the virtuoso's temptation to love material perfection for its own sake. His technical skill always served his feelings and his emotions, and yet this desire to express the external world resulted in what one may well describe as pure painting, because it found its justification in itself and in the reasons we have for admiring it.

Paradoxically, the ideas, the science of this tenacious man who followed his own path without letting side-issues deflect him, make a certain impression of awkwardness. His concern for perfection, his minute attention to details which he was continually retouching, correcting or improving, gives the impression of a perpetually changing art. His rejection of intellectual affectation is displayed in complex compositions and images which provoke thought — the slow and silent dialogue between the work and those who look at it. His respect for his subject when portraying people and their private, daily lives led him to be one of those painters in whom one might suppose that the idea of pure painting did not exclude representing material reality. Through the pure pleasure given by contemplating one of his pictures, he tends to make one forget the subject, or rather to make one understand that it is of secondary importance, though not completely negligible.

Everywhere one perceives his love of intimate dialogue, and his rejection of external extravagance in which so many other painters have hoped to find the noise and movement of the crowd. Bonnard's society is leisured and introspective; he never bears witness to a creative activity, whether that of a peasant, a workman or a man of his own class. He only wants to acknowledge man in his moments of relaxation, surrounded by the trappings of leisure.

Etching for "Saint Monica"

Etching for "Saint Monica"

Madame Nana Winding, 1942   Graphite, 19″ × 13″   The Lefevre Gallery, London

Perhaps it is this feeling which gives his art a feminine touch, because he belonged to a society in which a woman's life was primarily concerned with the exploitation of leisure, and kept pace with suitable occupations and thoughts. We may venture to assert that by this path he reached his high spiritual level, because the happy, expansive leisure which breathes through all Bonnard's work answers to a profound human need, and has an inner richness which does not need brilliant, importunate technical tricks to fill a void or arouse emotion at the presence of man.

Raymond Cogniat

CIRCUS HORSE, 1936-46   Canvas, 36½″ × 46″   Private Collection

BIOGRAPHY

BIOGRAPHY

1867 Born, on 3rd October, at Fontenay-aux-Roses, son of Eugène Bonnard, an official at the Ministry of War, and of Elisabeth Mertzdorff, an Alsatian from Thann.

1875 Studied at Vanves, then at Louis le Grand and then at Charlemagne.

1887 Having taken his degree in law, entered the Julian Academy and the School of Fine Arts. Made friends with Vuillard, Roussel, Maurice Denis, Sérusier, Ranson and Vallotton.

1888 Sérusier brought back from Brittany the picture he had painted at the instigation of Gauguin. The group of friends took the name of "nabis".

1889 Bonnard failed to obtain the Prix de Rome, and also failed in his attempts at an administrative career, being rejected at the competitive oral examination for registration. Settled into his first studio at the Batignolles. Sold a poster on the subject of "France-Champagne".

1890 Moved to a studio at 28 Rue Pigalle, with Vuillard and Maurice Denis. His young sister married the composer Claude Terrasse.

1891 Met Toulouse-Lautrec when his *France-Champagne* poster was published. Exhibited nine paintings at the Salon des Indépendants. First exhibition of the nabis at the Gallery Le Barc de Boutteville, in December. The "Revue Blanche" came to Paris.

1892 New exhibitions at the Salon des Indépendants and also exhibited with his friends at Le Barc de Boutteville.

1893 Same exhibitions. Illustrations for *The Little Tonic Sol-fa* and the *Little Family Scenes* by Claude Terrasse. Lithographs in the "Escarmouche" and the "Revue Blanche". Foundation of the Théâtre de l'Œuvre (Workshop Theatre). Met Vollard. New studio at 65 Rue de Douai.

1894 First portrait of Marthe. At the "Revue Blanche" meetings met Mirbeau, Henri de Régnier, Jules Renard, Tristan Bernard, Marcel Schwob and Félix Fénéon. Poster for the "Revue Blanche"

1895 Album of twelve lithographs on *Some Aspects of Parisian Life*, published by Vollard. Designs for a stained-glass window and for dining-room furniture.

1896 First personal exhibition at Durand-Ruel of 54 paintings, posters and lithographs. Franc-Nohain, Claude Terrasse and Alfred Jarry founded the Théâtre des Pantins, which gave many marionette performances and for which Bonnard made dolls and illustrated the programme. Exhibition at the "Libre Esthétique" at Brussels, with Vuillard and Lautrec. Lithographs for a poster of the Salon des Cent, for the "Peintres Graveurs" and for the programme of "La Dernière Croisade" ("The Last Crusade") at the Workshop Theatre.

1897 From now on exhibited regularly at the Salon des Indépendants and at the group exhibitions of his friends, both in France and abroad.

1904 Took part in a group exhibition at Bernheim-Jeune's Gallery, as a result of which this Gallery organized several private exhibitions for him from 1906 on.

1906 Travelled in Belgium and Holland.

1907 Travelled to England.

1908 Travelled in Italy, Algeria and Tunisia.

1909 First stay in the South of France, at St. Tropez, which he revisited during the following years.

1912 Bought a house "My Caravan", near Vernon. Met Monet at Giverny.

1913 Travelled to Hamburg.

1925 Bought a little house "The Grove" at Cannet.

1926 Visit to the United States, on the occasion of the award to him of the Carnegie Prize.

1934 Large exhibition at the Wildenstein Gallery in New York.

1936 Received a second Carnegie Prize.

1939 Retired to Cannet.

1942 Marthe Bonnard died.

1947 23rd January. Died at Cannet.

BIBLIOGRAPHY

BOOKS ILLUSTRATED BY BONNARD

TERRASSE, Claude. *Little Family Scenes for the Piano.* Fromont. Paris 1892.

TERRASSE, Claude. *The Illustrated Tonic Sol-fa.* Quantin. Paris 1893.

NANSEN, Peter. *Marie.* La Revue Blanche. Paris 1898.

JARRY, Alfred. *The Little Almanach of Père Ubu.* Paris 1899.

VERLAINE, Paul. *In Parallel.* Vollard. Paris 1902.

LONGUS. *Daphnis and Chloë.* Vollard. Paris 1902.

RENARD, Jules. *Natural History.* Flammarion. Paris 1904.

MIRBEAU, Octave. *The 628 E 8.* Charpentier et Fasquelle. Paris 1908.

BARRUCAND, Victor. *From a Lovelier Country.* Floury. Paris 1910.

GIDE, André. *Prometheus Badly Bound.* NRF. Paris 1920.

ANET, Claude. *Notes on Love.* Crès. Paris 1922.

CHAUVEAU, Léopold. *History of the Hammer-fish and the Sword-fish.* Payot. Paris 1923.

GOMEZ DE LA SERNA, R. *Breasts.* Crès. Paris 1924.

MIRBEAU, Octave. *Dingo.* Vollard. Paris 1924.

CHAUVEAU, Léopold. *History of the Little Renaud.* NRF. Paris 1927.

ROGER-MARX, Claude. *Simili.* Au Sans Pareil. Paris 1930.

VOLLARD, Ambroise. *The Life of Saint Monica.* Vollard. Paris 1930.

BONNARD, Pierre. *Correspondence.* Tériade. Paris 1945.

LOUYS, Pierre. *The Twilight of the Nymphs.* Pierre Tisné. Paris 1946.

COLETTE. *Beautiful Seasons.* Club des Lecteurs de la Gazette des Lettres. Paris 1947.

BOOKS ON BONNARD

WERTH, Léon. *Bonnard.* Collection: Les Cahiers d'Aujourd'hui. Paris 1919.

FOSCA, François. *Bonnard.* Kundig, Geneva and Crès. Paris 1919.

COQUIOT, Gustave. *Bonnard.* Bernheim Jeune. Paris 1922.

ROGER-MARX, Claude. *Pierre Bonnard.* NRF. Paris 1924.

TERRASSE, Claude. *Bonnard.* Floury. Paris 1927.

BESSON, George. *Bonnard.* Braun. Paris 1934.

LOTHE, André. *Sixteen Paintings by Bonnard.* Editions du Chêne. Paris 1944.

DE LAPRADE, Jacques. *Bonnard.* Braun. Paris 1944.

COURTHION, Pierre. *Bonnard, the Painter of Wonders.* Marguerat. Lausanne 1945.

JOURDAIN, Francis. *Bonnard, or the Virtues of Freedom.* Skira. Geneva 1946.

BEER, François Joachim. *Pierre Bonnard.* Editions Françaises d'Art. Marseille 1947.

REWALD, John. *Pierre Bonnard.* Museum of Modern Art. New York 1948.

ROGER-MARX, Claude. *Bonnard.* Hazan. Paris 1950.

NATANSON, Thadée. *My Ideas on Bonnard.* Cailler. Geneva 1951.

ROGER-MARX, Claude. *Bonnard the Lithographer.* André Sauret. Monaco 1952.

TERRASSE, Antoine. *Bonnard.* Skira. Geneva 1964.

BOURET, Jean. *Bonnard.* Bibliothèque des Artes. Paris 1967.

TERRASSE, Antoine. *Pierre Bonnard.* Gallimard. Paris 1967.

ILLUSTRATIONS